Musées (

C000183585

HAUTEVILLE HOUSE

general guide

Summary

I am told that your house reflects your soul in its elevation and poetry, and that you feel at home amid the roar of the wind and the waves. (Charles Baudelaire to Victor Hugo, 27th September 1859.)

On 31st October 1855, a large crowd greeted Victor Hugo as he arrived in St. Peter Port, the capital of Guernsey, with his son François-Victor. They moved into the Hôtel de l'Europe, accompanied by Juliette Drouet. The poet had just been expelled from Jersey, following the publication of Félix Pyat's letter criticising Queen Victoria's visit to France in the local exiles' newspaper, *L'Homme*.

His elder son Charles joined them on 2nd November, followed on 9th November by his wife and daughter, both named Adèle, and by Auguste Vacquerie[1]. That same day, the family moved into a house at n° 20 rue de Hauteville, which the poet had rented for a minimum of one year, containing some rather precarious items of furniture, also rented.

This first house is either referred to as Hauteville-Terrace, after Marine-Terrace, their Jersey home, or already by the name Hauteville House.

I live in a seagull's nest high above the town ; from my window I overlook the entire archipelago of the Channel ; I can see France from which I am banished, and Jersey from which I am expelled ; [...][2].

[...] Imagine my state of mind living in such splendid solitude, as though perched on the pinnacle of a rock, with all the great foaming waves and huge scudding clouds below my window. I live in this immense ocean dream, gradually turning into a sleepwalker of the sea, and, before all these breathtaking images and the vast living thoughts which engulf me, I end up merely being a kind of witness of God[3].

On 16th May 1856, with the proceeds from *Les Contemplations*, published in April and immediately sold out, Victor Hugo gave William Ozanne 24 000 francs for a house situated slightly further up the same street, at n° 38. It was reputedly haunted. The status of home-owner protected him

from any threat of eviction, although he did find himself having to pay the Queen an annual hen tax, a feudal practice which exacted the gift of two hens or the equivalent sum.

> *Picture me in the throes of virtually building a house ; failing a homeland, I must at least have a roof. [...]This time, if I am hounded out again, I want to make honest and prurient Albion commit a drastic act ; I want to see it trample on a man's home, the famous English castle and sacred haven of each citizen.*

> *Strangely enough this political experience has been made possible through literature. The Guernsey house [...] owes its existence to* Les Contemplations. *I owe everything to this book, from the very first beam to the very last tile. It has given me a roof [...]*[4].

> *Here am I, representative of the people and banished soldier of the French Republic, paying an annual hen tax to the Queen of England, ruler of the Channel Islands, in her capacity as Duchess of Normandy and my feudal suzerain. This is just one of the eccentric consequences of exile*[5].

The poet did briefly consider naming his new home Liberty House but finally opted for Hauteville House.

The house was built at the turn of the century by a privateer. It was surrounded by a sizeable garden, and was ideally located overlooking the harbour and Cornet Castle.

Mulling
*Victor Hugo
and his two sons,
Charles and
François-Victor*
1860

Work started on the house almost immediately and on 5th November 1856 the family moved in, against a chaotic background of men at work. They had already begun alterations on the top floor by building a belvedere overlooking the garden in what was to become Victor Hugo's bedroom, and creating servants' quarters with casement windows. Victor Hugo had also given instructions for a balustrade to be built around the roof.

On 17th October 1856, Adèle Hugo gave vent to her anxiety in a letter to Mme Paul Meurice : [...] *I am also most unhappy ; we are about to move into our house, and this only seems to confirm our state of exile* [...] *I will surely die here.* [...]

It is not that I believe that the situation will last indefinitely in France ; but my husband is bound to settle in here. He will arrange the house according to personal taste, furnish it in the same way as his Parisian homes, and it will bear no kind of resemblance to a country retreat, those accidental houses of such modest and unpretentious aspect that they leave one free. Here my husband places his gilt and hangings and all his imagination and care. Once more we find ourselves attached to the walls. We are spending a lot of money and even if there arose an opportunity of going home, there would be none left to equip anywhere else.

In August 1859, Victor Hugo categorically refused the amnesty decree issued by Napoleon III, and Adèle's fears were realised. The poet settled into exile. He spent most of the following long years at Hauteville House, a period which only ended with the fall of the Empire. On 27th June 1861, he wrote to Noël Parfait from Belgium : *As for me, I am a storm bird. I am beginning to feel the need for clouds, seaspray and hurricanes. I would find it difficult now to live in the city full-time. I would become nostalgic for the ocean.*

Even in isolation, Victor Hugo managed to maintain his immense prestige, keeping up a prolific correspondence despite censorship. Publications followed on one another. *La Légende des siècles* in 1859, *Les Misérables* (started in the Place Royale, abandoned in 1848 and taken up again in 1860) in 1862, *William Shakespeare* in 1864, *Les Chansons des rues et des bois* in 1865, *Les Travailleurs de la mer* in 1866, *Le Paris Guide*, for which Victor Hugo wrote the introduction, and *La Voix de Guernesey* in 1867, *L'Homme qui rit* in 1869. Other works were written in Guernsey but only published later : in 1858 *La Pitié suprême* and *L'Ane*, in 1866 *Mille francs de récompense*, in 1867 *Mangeront-ils ?*, in 1869 *L'Epée* and *Torquemada*. He also made a vast number of public interventions and declarations.

Within the context of exile, family life got itself organised and everyone set about their own occupations. Adèle I made the most of these years to write a book of memoirs on Victor Hugo, published in June 1863 under the title *Victor Hugo raconté par un témoin de sa vie*. Charles painted and wrote novels and plays, François-Victor took on the task of translating the works of Shakespeare, published between 1858 and 1865. Adèle II played the piano and tried her hand at composing.

The passing years radically altered family harmony, however, and Victor Hugo found himself alone in Hauteville House for long periods.

From 1868 on, Adèle I tried to distract her daughter from the stifling atmosphere of life in exile by taking her away for several months at a time to Paris, London and Brussels.

On 18th June 1863, Adèle II, whose mental health had deteriorated with the years, left Hauteville House for ever. She had fallen desperately in love with Lieutenant Pinson, whom she had met in Guernsey, and pursued him as far as Halifax in Canada. On 17th October 1863, *La Gazette de Guernesey* published the inaccurate announcement of their marriage. In 1866, Adèle followed Pinson's regiment to Barbados, a small island in the British West Indies. Throughout these years, Victor Hugo, from Guernsey, supported his daughter financially, still hoping for her return. But Adèle was only brought back from Barbados to Paris in February 1872, to be admitted to a mental hospital in Saint-Mandé.

Adèle I's absences became increasingly frequent and prolonged. She made lengthy trips to Paris and Brussels, finally settling there in 1865 to be near her two sons. Charles had left Guernsey in 1861 and moved to Brussels, where he married the young Alice Lehaene in October 1865, and their two children, Georges and Jeanne, were born there in 1868 and 1869. François-Victor, who found life in Guernsey intolerable following the death of his fiancée Emily de Putron in January 1865, joined his brother in Brussels, where their mother died on 27th August 1868.

Victor Hugo's loneliness was tempered by the loyalty and constant presence of Juliette Drouet. On 19th December 1857, she moved into La Fallue, and from her windows could see the poet several times a day. On 15th June 1864, she moved to n° 20 Hauteville, where the Hugo family had spent their first year in exile in Guernsey. Her new home was christened Hauteville Fairy. The purchase was shared half and half between herself and Victor Hugo and she retained the usufruct. It was furnished and decorated by the poet himself, who gave the house the benefit of his considerable talents.

Julie Chenay, Victor Hugo's sister-in-law, was a frequent visitor to Hauteville House, finally moving in. She often looked after the house during the long summer trips to Belgium, Holland,

Arsène Garnier
Victor Hugo
and his family
in the garden
1856-1860

Luxembourg and the Rhineland undertaken by Victor Hugo and Juliette Drouet from 1861, and remained at Hauteville House once the poet had returned to France.

On 15th August 1870, having filed away all his manuscripts, Victor Hugo, accompanied by Juliette Drouet, left Guernsey for Brussels. On 5th September, the poet's triumphant return to Paris marked the end of an exile which had lasted nearly nineteen years, fifteen of them spent in Guernsey.

Victor Hugo returned to Guernsey on three occasions, accompanied by Juliette Drouet.

From 9th August 1872 to 30th July 1873 he paid a lengthy visit, during which he wrote *Quatrevingt-treize*. He was forced to return to Paris because of the serious illness of François-Victor, who died on 26th December 1873.

He came back for a week from 20th to 27th April 1875, in order to reclaim the trunk crammed with his notes and files, which he had left in the Bank of Guernsey in August 1870.

His final visit, to convalesce after a stroke, took place between 5th July and 9th November 1878.

The plain, flat street façade, with its sash windows, provides no clue to the opulent interior decoration, the result of many years work, minutely orchestrated by the master of the house.

In Guernsey, Victor Hugo was able to indulge in his well-known passion for bric-à-brac and interior decoration, which had struck his contemporaries long before his exile. Accompanied by Juliette Drouet and a certain Grut, he scoured the island from end to end, returning from these expeditions with a rich harvest of sideboards and chests (over sixty in 1857 and early 1858), panels and furnishings. *Hunt for old chests*, he writes over and over in his notebooks. During this period he began buying numerous items such as figurines, mirrors, tiles, carpets, pictures, lamps... All these elements gradually found a home. Meanwhile, thanks to the diligence of Paul Meurice, a loyal friend to Victor Hugo, and to

Auguste Vacquerie, cases of furniture left before the departure into exile were arriving from Paris. The purchases continued over a long period. Victor Hugo also made the most of his annual journeys to unearth curiosities in London or in Brussels, sometimes asking his sons to do likewise. *The good fairy Bric-à-Brac has smiled on me and god Trinket befriended me ; I gleaned a number of unusual objects in Brussels, for little money. [...] One is absolutely unique and impossible to find. I found it*[6].

      With Mauger as foreman and three workmen, Tom Gor, Jean and James, work continued at a snail's pace, much to Victor Hugo's irritation. *My house is still being built nail by nail. One refers to the caution of slowness, but the folly of slowness would be more apposite in the case of the Guernsey workman*[7] *[...]. My house is still no more than a hut ; it has been taken over by solid Guernsey workmen, who, believing me to be rich, find it only fair to exploit «the great Frenchman» a little and drag out the work and the pleasure for as long as possible. Nevertheless I tell myself that the house will be finished one day, and that you may then, in the course of time and space, feel an inclination to come and consecrate some little corner by your presence and memory. What is your opinion of such fond illusions ?* [8]

      The poet made a great number of preparatory sketches and drawings for this house, which was an original product of his own fertile imagination, and he supervised their realisation with great care. His signature or initials can be found in every room. The phenomenal activity he displayed during this period is obvious from a letter he sent to François-Victor on 15th August 1859 : *As for me, I am standing on a quadriga, as I write* Les Chansons des rues et des bois*, print* La Légende des siècles*, conjure up the drama* Torquemada *and spur on Mauger. I drive all four monsters with tremendous gusto.*

      The task spanned a period between 1857 and late 1859, and its details are well-known to us thanks to Victor Hugo's notebooks, which he kept meticulously up to date. [...] *for the moment everything is finished in the house*, he wrote on 5th December 1859.

In May 1857, the dining room was inaugurated. The billiard room was completed in March 1858, the tapestry room and entrance hall lobby in May, the studio in September, the china corridor and staircase in December. Meanwhile conversion work was in progress in the red and blue drawing rooms and on the first-floor landing, which was finished in March 1858, and work was being carried out on the landing-library and oak gallery. In the summer of 1858, they began equipping the third floor (the lobby and Victor Hugo's bedroom).

Mauger died on 19th January 1860. Peace returned for several months until the ground-floor bathroom was installed in July of the same year.

In late 1861, Victor Hugo totally transformed the third floor by having a look-out or glass room built on the roof. The glass cone above the stairwell was replaced by a transparent slab, which became the floor of the new room.

This fascinating abode soon aroused interest. On 31st July 1859, Victor Hugo wrote to his wife : *People are beginning to be drawn here through curiosity. But I keep the door closed as much as possible.*

In 1863 an anonymous work appeared, actually written by Charles Hugo, entitled *Chez Victor Hugo par un passant* : *[...] the distinguishing aspect of this house, apart from the curious and highly personal style of decoration, is the quantity of mottoes and inscriptions visible everywhere on the furniture and the walls, all of them the unpublished thoughts of Victor Hugo. One can therefore foresee that his Guernsey home will one day form for his biographers a virtual autograph on three floors, somewhat like a poem in several rooms, if one can put it that way[9].*

As early as June 1861, Charles Hugo had suggested to the publisher Hetzel bringing out a brochure on Hauteville House. During the summer of 1862, the photographer Edmond Bacot brought back fifty-seven plates from his two-week stay in Hauteville House, and several of these were engraved by Maxime Lalanne to illustrate Charles Hugo's book.

Victor Hugo
*Decorative
composition*

There was no shortage of tourists wishing to visit Hauteville House. During the final years of exile, they are frequently referred to in the notebooks. On 19th October 1867 Victor Hugo writes : *Apparently Marie*[10] *earned over 200 francs during my absence by showing my house to the curious* and on the following day he wrote to François-Victor : *[...] almost one thousand foreign visitors came to Hauteville-House this summer. When I arrived I had to go through a register full of names and comments. There was a plethora of English colonels and American reverends.*

On 26th November 1863, Victor Hugo wrote to Maxime Lalanne : *I left Paris twelve years ago somewhat as one abandons ship ; I managed to save some of the flotsam, which I arranged about me as best I could in my Guernsey home. It is this modest achievement that you have turned into a work of art.* This *modest achievement*, still visible today, offers a unique and fascinating insight into the inexhaustible creative energy of Victor Hugo.

1. A close friend of the family, whose brother Charles had married Léopoldine Hugo in 1843.

2. Letter from Victor Hugo to Hetzel, 27th November 1855.

3. Letter from Victor Hugo to Franz Stevens, 10th April 1856.

4. Letter from Victor Hugo to Jules Janin, 16th August 1856.

5. Letter from Victor Hugo to Octave Lacroix, 30th June 1862.

6. Letter from Victor Hugo to François-Victor, 22nd April 1861.

7. Letter from Victor Hugo to Paul Meurice, 17th May 1857.

8. Letter from Victor Hugo to George Sand, 28th May 1858.

9. This quotation is taken from the manuscript of the work *Chez Victor Hugo par un passant avec 12 eaux-fortes par M. Maxime Lalanne*, Paris. The manuscript is preserved in the Maison de Victor Hugo.

10. Marie Sixty, the servant.

THE ENTRANCE HALL

Below the words Hauteville House in translucid lettering, the front door opens directly into the entrance hall lobby.

Directly in line with the the door is the porch of Notre-Dame de Paris, which immediately plunges the visitor into the atmosphere of the house and recalls the importance of the Middle Ages in Victor Hugo's inspiration. Charles Hugo refers to it as the *frontispiece of Hauteville House*[1]. A fluted column with a Corinthian capital, resting on a square pillar decorated with a plant motif, put in by Mauger in June 1858, supports a composition with an embossed stained glass base which barely allows the light to filter through. Bottle bases are used in this way again elsewhere. In the centre, beneath the inscription *VICTOR HUGO / [N]OSTRE-DAME DE PARIS*, terracotta sculptures recall the novel, published in 1831, and evoke the frontispiece drawn by Célestin Nanteuil in 1833. There are still traces of the gilt which once covered some parts. This composition probably corresponds to a mirror which hung in the smaller drawing room of Victor Hugo's apartment in the rue de la Tour-d'Auvergne in Paris, before he went into exile. On either side, inserted into the wood panelling, are two medallions by David d'Angers representing the young Victor Hugo and his daughter Adèle, the latter dated 1845. One remarks a small head with flamboyant hair gracing the capital. This detail frequently recurs in the panelling of the house, both on the ground floor and in the oak gallery.

In May 1858 the walls and ceiling were covered with plant-patterned wallpaper. This completed this section of the lobby.

On the other side of the Notre-Dame de Paris porch one can see the inscription *AMA CREDE* (Love. Believe) on the upper lintel. Hauteville House is full of inscriptions of this kind, engraved in wood, sometimes painted, mottoes and maxims placed here and there by the poet.

　　　　The visitor steps into the hall. To the left, a sales counter is located on the site of Auguste Vacquerie's former bedroom. He was a frequent visitor to Guernsey.

　　　　To the right, a double door, completed on 29th January 1858, opens into the billiard room. The door is made up of two wooden panels with stylised flower carvings, a recurring theme in the interior decoration of Hauteville House. Single partitions at the base of each panel have transformed them into doors. This ensemble, perfectly integrated into the pannelling which covers the right-hand wall of the hall, is topped by a polychrome and gilt Virgin and Child, placed there on 16th July 1859. The inscription *AVE*, carved into the wood in the centre of the door, stands out from a double blazon to welcome the visitor.

1. CHARLES HUGO, *op. cit.*

THE BILLIARD ROOM

The billiard table, which takes up much of the room, was bought by Victor Hugo in February 1857.

On the walls are several copies of pictures, the originals of which hang in the Maison de Victor Hugo in Paris : Adèle Hugo by Louis Boulanger (1839 Salon) ; Victor Hugo circa 1833 by Louis Boulanger ; Victor Hugo and his son François-Victor by Auguste de Châtillon (1836 Salon) ; Léopoldine aged four by Louis Boulanger ; General Léopold Hugo ; François-Victor circa 1834 by Charles de Champmartin.

Two paintings by Louis Boulanger can be seen : the small portrait of Léopoldine as a child, wearing a white bonnet, and another of her sister Adèle, sitting in a large red armchair.

Facing the door, a picture by Saint-Evre depicts *Inez de Castro*. This work, which formerly adorned the drawing-room of the place Royale, was given to Victor Hugo by the Duke and Duchess of Orléans, on the publication of *Les Voix intérieures*, shortly after the celebrations held by the King in Versailles to mark the opening of the historical museum commemorating France's glorious achievements. Victor Hugo had been presented to the Duchess of Orléans on this occasion. A reminder of the pre-exile years, this picture features among the few belongings which escaped the auction of Victor Hugo's furniture organised in Paris on 8th and 9th June 1852. The poet, meanwhile, was in Brussels, where he had sought refuge on 12th December 1851.

Two portraits of Léopoldine Hugo have been placed here. One, in its original studded red velvet frame, is a replica of the portrait executed in 1842-1843 by Edouard Dubufe, now preserved in Paris at the Maison de Victor Hugo and the other, in an oval frame, is a work by Mme Hugo. The latter also painted the portrait of her younger son, François-Victor, signed and dated *1847*, and also the one of her daughter Adèle, in its original studded red velvet frame.

Two other graphite drawings are worth noting, by Julie Duvidal de Montferrier, the wife of Abel, Victor Hugo's eldest brother : a self-portrait and a portrait of Mme Hugo. Julie Duvidal de Montferrier, a pupil of Baron Gérard, gave drawing lessons to the young Adèle Foucher before her marriage to Victor Hugo.

The fireplace in this room is made up of veneered wood panelling placed over the marble mantel. A carved panel featuring a small cherub's head in the centre closes the hearth. Two Chippendale chairs complete the decor. In Victor Hugo's time there was also a large divan, similar to those in the tapestry room and studio, draped in rugs.

In the poet's day a number of his own drawings hung on the walls, including a series with frames adorned by him with floral decorations in November 1859. Most of these drawings are preserved in the Maison de Victor Hugo.

In 1866, the billiard room was closed off and padlocked by order of Victor Hugo. Boxes crammed with objects still in their wrappings were stocked there. It was only after the poet's death that the room was used for its original purpose.

A double door, topped by a battle scene, leads to the tapestry room.

THE TAPESTRY ROOM

This room and the ones which follow have retained all their original decor. This is where the family gathered. *We danced in the tapestry room until 4 in the morning* noted Victor Hugo on 28th August 1860.

On this side, the double door communicating with the billiard room is decorated with an opulent carved decor. On the upper part two medallions face one another. Just below the ceiling is a chair back with a carved horseman, over the rectangular panel above the door. Victor Hugo bought this on 9th July 1857, on one of his expeditions to *hunt for old chests*. On either side, set within two coats of arms, are the engraved inscriptions *BON / ROY-ROY / QUI / S'EN VA*.

One is immediately struck by the vast sideboard, centred upon a Delft fireplace with a blue and white design, which almost fills an entire wall. On the mantel, framed by embossed winged caryatids in relief alternating with embossed masks, one can see painted medallions adorned with angels, a flower basket or wreath in their hand, or a trumpet to their lips. The amazing composition, which serves to encase the hearth, is a perfect example of Hugo's concept of decoration. The poet visualised ensembles of this kind using elements gleaned here and there, drafted various projects and then passed them on to Mauger to create.

The upper part, with a projecting centre crowned by a pediment, is made up of three distinct chests with hinged panels. A number of floral designs featured in the hall crop up again here. The statuette of the bishop on the pediment is flanked by two inscriptions engraved upon coats of arms : *CROSSE / D'OR / EVESQUE / DE BOIS-CROSSE / DE BOIS / EVESQUE / D'OR.*

The convex mirror which reflects the tapestry illustrates the important rôle of reflection in the poet-decorator's vision. There are numerous plays on mirrors and transparency in Hauteville House.

Four rotund columns appear to support the central chest. The two back columns have been cut in half. On either side are two wooden statues bought by Charles Hugo in London in May 1859 : St. Paul holding a book on the left, and St. John gazing heavenwards on the right. *Mauger has put in the two statuettes for the fireplace on which I have written* : *IN LIBRO. AD COELUM* noted Victor Hugo on 16th June 1859. The two vases were bought in January 1862.

The layout of the lower part of the sideboard, with the fireplace recessed, is in stark contrast to the upper part. The decor is less opulent. Two volutes bear engraved inscriptions, some of which are difficult to make out. On the left *JOB / ISAIE / HOMERE / ESCHYLE / LUCRECE / DANTE / SHASPEARE* [sic] / *MOLIERE*. On the right *MOISE / SOCRATE / CHRIST / COLOMB / LUTHER / WASHINGTON*. Beneath the scrolls, like a signature, the two interwoven letters *V H* are embossed in the wood. The decorator's stamp reappears on the lower part, under the lozenges placed on either side of the fireplace. At the corners are the two familiar small fluted columns.

On either side, against a tapestry background, are two long mirrors, their stains painted over with flowers by Charles in April 1858.

On the wall opposite this unusual piece hangs an XVIIIth century Aubusson tapestry depicting a hunting scene. It was placed there on 19th February 1858 after the door communicating with the china corridor had been walled up. Mauger carved its wooden frame. In the lower corners one can see the shields adorned on the left with the arms of the Lorraine Hugos, from whom the poet believed he descended, and on the right with those of General Léopold Hugo, Victor Hugo's father, who was made Count under the Empire following his victory over a Spanish guerilla leader, in July 1810, at Sigüenza.

A small plaque bearing the words *NOBLE PLAY* has been fixed beneath the tapestry. These are the only English words to be found in the house. Norman patois was spoken in Guernsey and Victor Hugo himself never learned any English. He only knew the odd word, and these crop up here and there in his correspondence or notebooks, sometimes deliberately phonetically transcribed. His son François-Victor, who spoke English perfectly, was invaluable to him when Adèle fled to Canada and during the long period in Halifax.

Above this tapestry, at cornice level, one can see the inscription *LAETUS HOMO RIDET FLET BESTIA TRISTIS* (Satisfied, man laughs, the beast is sad and weeps).

A large settee draped in an Oriental rug runs along the wall. The notebooks register frequent purchases of carpets, sometimes in fragments. They were cut out and resewn according to Victor Hugo's instructions and then adapted on to divans, simple wooden frames he had made on the spot. On 12th April 1858 : *Marie Turpin*[1] *[...] has started cutting out the Turkish carpet to cover the divan in the downstairs drawing-room.*

Tapestries are omnipresent in this room. The ones placed on either side of the door to the billiard room, an offering to Pan and a verdure depicting a parrot, both XVIII th century, were hung in February 1858. A number of fragments have been cut out and inserted into the wood panelling. To the right of the window, over the two superposed cabinets, the peony and bird tapestry is framed by a set-in border.

The table in the centre is another of Hugo's creations. A wide wooden band has been added to the table top to enlarge it. *We have finished the table of the tapestry room* wrote Victor Hugo on 3rd December 1858. The Chippendale chairs around it resemble the ones in the billiard room.

The large XVIIIth century tapestry on the ceiling was laid by Jean and James on 9th February 1858. By 17th, the ensemble was completed. One cannot but be struck by the layout of the ceiling, which has been completely covered over, with carved panels and pieces of tapestry acting as a frame for the central section. The technique is taken up again in the studio, the dining room and the oak gallery.

To the left of the sizeable sideboard-fireplace, a door concealed in the pannelling leads to a small room which was used as a photographic studio by Charles and Auguste Vacquerie. This is the famous darkroom, to be immortalised much later in one of the most famous poems of *L'Art d'être grand-père* (VI, 6) :

Jeanne était au pain sec dans le cabinet noir,
Pour un crime quelconque, et, manquant au devoir,
J'allai voir la proscrite en pleine forfaiture,
Et lui glissai dans l'ombre un pot de confiture
Contraire aux lois. [...]

Above the door leading to the studio, which was made from the leaves of a cupboard, are two Chinese rice paper «slides», inserted on 7th April 1858, and visible from both sides.

1. The servant.

The visitor now steps into the different atmosphere of the studio or smoking-room, which overlooks the garden and is lit by a large bay window.

Once again, one is drawn by the vast sideboard, designed by the poet, which fills an entire wall and brings into play an already familiar decorative repertoire. The central part is made up of three elongated panels, adorned with hinges, on which Victor Hugo's coats of arms feature once again : those of the Lorraine Hugos on the left, and the General's on the right. Overhead, the two small rotund columns evoke those of the sideboard-fireplace in the tapestry room. They appear to support the two-doored sideboard of the upper part, on which the recurring motif of a small, sometimes winged, head appears. On either side, beneath two wooden vases, are two chest elements resting on fluted columns, similar to those in the porch of Notre-Dame de Paris. The seven-branch chandelier seen here turns up again in the dining room. On the right, a small stepladder, also decorated with a winged head, introduces a utilitarian touch to the general effect.

Above the sideboard, half hidden by the moulding, the inscription *AD AUGUSTA PER ANGUSTA* (Towards elevated goals via narrow paths) was traced by Mauger in May 1859. This was the conspirators' password in *Hernani*.

Beneath the window, a divan draped in an Oriental rug incites one to rest. Two stained glass panels are worth noting, surrounded by yellow-orange glass. The upper cartouche, with an inscription in Dutch, bears the date *1669*, and below two interwoven *grisaille* bells are framed by a foliate scroll.

The furniture is completed by a *meuble à deux corps*, a lacquered clock case bought on 7th November 1863 and a wooden travelling chest.

In the centre of the room is an octagonal table, its legs carved by Grut in 1857. At the cincture, two fauns and two female figures are etched in windows hollowed out from the wood. Stylised plant designs adorn the legs.

On the table top, a yellow varnished pottery vase, bought by Victor Hugo on 26th February 1864, bears the engraved motto *HONY SOET QUI MAL Y PENSE* and the date *1760*.

On the walls are two oval monochrome painted medallions on a gold background : to the left of the door, Bacchus, to the left of the large sideboard, the goat Amaltheia eia.

The whole ceiling has been covered in the same way as the tapestry room. A large Flemish tapestry, *La Leçon de musique*, is framed with fragments from other tapestries and carved panels.

A Chinese lantern with fretwork motifs lights the room.

THE CHINA CORRIDOR

The visitor now returns to the entrance hall. The china corridor, directly in line with the porch of Notre-Dame de Paris, opens out ahead, communicating with the garden.

Victor Hugo fitted racks into the walls and ceiling of this passageway, transforming it into a kind of large dresser, with a red background designed to show off the china and porcelain. The layout inevitably calls to mind the Chinese drawing room created several years later by the poet, in 1863-1864, for Hauteville Fairy, Juliette Drouet's house. The decor for the latter has since been reconstituted in the Maison de Victor Hugo.

On the left-hand wall hangs a Sèvres porcelain service with a gold decoration, given to the poet by the King in June 1825, in recognition of his ode on *Le sacre de Charles X*. On the right, among other items, is a polychrome bone china service by the English manufacturer Mason, mentioned several times in the notebooks.

The ceiling is composed of dishes from a variety of sources, picked up here and there by Victor Hugo and arranged around the lid of a Rouen china soup tureen. The bowl is displayed in the dining-room.

The far door opens on to the garden, carefully tended by Victor Hugo. In the centre a vase-shaped fountain is reflected in the water, with the words *UBI SPES IBI PAX* (Where there is hope there is peace) and *17 OCTOBRE 1856 V.H.* engraved into the plinth. Ivy once covered the base. The fountain used to adorn the garden of the Rohan-Guéménée mansion in the place Royale, where the family lived from 1832 to 1848. Victor Hugo purchased it in August 1847.

Un vase en terre cuite, en style rococo,
Dans l'eau qui tremble avec de confuses cadences,
Mire les deux serpents qui lui tiennent lieu d'anses,
Et qui jadis voyaient danser dans leur réduit
Les marquises le jour, les dryades la nuit.
(Dernière Gerbe, XVIII.)

On either side are two china dragons with only their heads left.

The garden, which contained an aviary, completed in June 1857, a greenhouse with a vine in it, and a vegetable plot, was planted with aloes, growing not far from the fountain, eucalyptus, climbing fruit trees, laburnum, lilac and osier... At the far end, an arbour once graced an alley of fig trees, later torn down by a hurricane and replaced by grass, and this is where Victor Hugo sat in the shade during the summer of 1869 to write *Torquemada*. On the lawn is a reed, together with a profusion of shrubs, azaleas, lavender, lily, roses, rhododendrons and fushchias..., all flourishing in the mild Guernsey climate. *My garden is filled with flowers* wrote Victor Hugo on 30th November 1872.

On 14th July 1870, *the oak of the United States of Europe* was planted, and is still standing today : *Today 14th July 1870, at one o'clock in the afternoon, with the help of my gardener Tourtell and in the presence of my son Charles, [...] Mme Charles Hugo, [...] Mme Chenay, [...] and with Little Georges and Little Jeanne there, I planted an acorn in my garden from which an oak will grow, christened by me* <u>Oak of the United States of Europe</u>. On the following 13th September, shortly after his return to Paris, Victor Hugo noted : *Julie has written from Guernsey to say that the acorn I planted on 14th July has sprouted. The oak of the United States of Europe emerged from the soil on 5th September, the day of my return to Paris.*

Along the right-hand wall, above a stone bench featuring a china chimaera similar to the ones in the red drawing room, the following line of poetry has been engraved : *IMMENSITE DIT L'ETRE ETERNITE DIT L'AME* (*Les Contemplations, Autrefois*, Book III, 30).

Edmond Bacot
Victor Hugo
in front of the
fountain
1862

THE DINING ROOM

Its entrance, in the hall, is marked by wooden coffering, engraved with the letters *V* and *H* on the bottom. Above it are two clock cases in ornamented wood. Over the smooth swing doors, gaslighting was provided by what Victor Hugo referred to as *the perystile* [sic] *bell lamp*. Above, the inscription *EGO HUGO* in interwoven letters can be made out.

The dining room was inaugurated on 14th May 1857, with a dinner for twenty-one guests. According to Charles Hugo, the room was nicknamed *salle à Mauger** [1]. Many of the preparatory sketches for the dining room have been preserved.

The swing doors were carved by Mauger in May 1858. The seven-branch chandelier seen on the sideboard in the studio turns up again here. On the upper part, a protruding section provides nooks for statuettes, adding a touch of grandeur to the whole effect. An inscription recalls that *EXILIUM VITA EST* (Life is an exile).

* Translator's note : a play on «salle à manger».

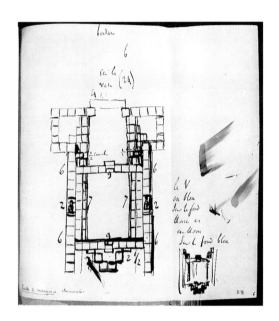

Victor Hugo
*Project for the
dining room
fieplace*

Above the wooden panelling, the walls are entirely
covered in Delft tiles, scrupulously laid out according to Victor
Hugo's wishes. The eleven purple bouquets were bought on 10th
November 1856 and placed there in April 1857. A frieze in the
same colour, illustrated with scenes from peasant life, forms the
border.

The decor reaches its culmination with the wall of the
fireplace, conceived by the poet-decorator. Here blue features
alongside purple. The projecting central element forms an
enormous double *H* (Hauteville House) above the hearth, closed
off by a painted still life. It is topped by a Virgin and Child,
NOTRE-DAME DE BON SECOURS, dated 1756, with a white
china mask supporting the plinth. The wooden panelling which
protrudes on either side of the statuette carries the inscription :
*LE PEUPLE EST PETIT MAIS IL SERA GRAND / DANS TES BRAS
SACRES O MERE FECONDE / O LIBERTE SAINTE AU PAS
CONQUERANT / TU PORTES L'ENFANT QUI PORTE LE MONDE.*

Victor Hugo
*Dining room
fireplace*

This wall decoration features several series of tiles including a number of biblical scenes.

The poet's signature appears in the corners of the fireplace : on the left, the tiles, some of them in *grisaille*, trace the interwoven *V* and *H*, on the right a blue *H*.

China items in various styles have been inserted here and there, sometimes placed on ceramic plinths, but more often inserted into the tiles. The Chinese drawing room designed for Hauteville Fairy comes to mind once more. On either side of the Virgin and Child, in the centre, are two Rouen china vases, and, between the downstrokes of the H, a dish of the same origin. On the left, one remarks a tripod salt cellar, in XVIIth century blue and white Italian china, to which Victor Hugo was particularly attached. Underneath, in a small nook, is a statuette of a weeping woman, made in England, entitled *WIDOW*. In the corner cant of the wall are a Nevers china inkstand decorated with initials and birds and a Delft china flower-holder adorned with a mask. To the right of the fireplace, on the cant, beneath a Rouen china vase, a dish featuring a man on horseback bearing the caption *HANIBAL / 1624* and an ancient Rouen china fountain have been placed. The bowl is the soup tureen, the lid of which was placed by Victor Hugo on the ceiling of the china corridor. On the wall, a Rouen china helmet-shaped pitcher and a small English statuette depicting a woman carrying a jug and barrel match the left-hand side.

This composition, its symmetry tempered by the somewhat fanciful arrangement of the china items, was the fruit of numerous studies and sketches, which show the decorator's hesitations and attempts to find the right number, position and colour for the tiles, and the appropriate choice of elements.

In the corners of the room, jambs carved with figurines border the shelved panelling. Half-way up are two mythological animals of Oriental origin, in wood-coloured paint, with only the legs of their riders visible.

Light from the garden floods in through two large windows topped by upturned chair backs. Several maxims stand out in painted gold letters against a red background. On the upper part of the left-hand window is written *HOMO*, and on the base of the bench, *LEVER A VI DINER A X / SOUPER A VI COUCHER A X / FAICT VIVRE L'HOMME X FOIS X*. The same layout is respected on the upper part of the right-hand window, with the word *DEUS*, and on the base of the bench, *POST CAENAM ST / ABIS SEU PASSUS M / ILLE MEABIS VALE* (After a meal, remain standing or walk a thousand paces. Take care of yourself). Between the windows, on the ceiling, is the word *POPULUS*. On the opposite wall, *PATRIA*.

A curious composition stands here, known as the ancestors' armchair, above which the engraved wording reads *CELLA / PATRUM / DEFUNCTORUM* (The sanctuary of deceased ancestors). A chain with traces of gilt is draped across the majestuous seat with its polychrome highlights and decorative inscriptions, preventing anyone from sitting down. On the upper part, in a shield, is the motto *HIC / NIHIL / ALIAS / ALIQUID* (Here nothing, elsewhere something), written by Victor Hugo on 19th February 1859. On the inside, beneath a golden plaque depicting Christ and the Samaritan, on either side of a wooden Virgin, is the maxim *PULVIS / ES-CINIS / SUM* (You are dust, I am ash). The Lorraine Hugo coat of arms turns up again, as well as the date *1534* and the motto *EGO HUGO*. Beneath the stylised flower, *ABSENTES ADSUNT* (The absent are present). On the outside of the right-hand armrest is written *GEORGES / 1534*, a reference to Hugo's earliest ancestor, and on the left-hand one *JOSEPH LEOPOLD SIGISBERT / 1828*, the poet's father, who died in 1828. The front of the seat also features the H of Hugo in relief.

Wooden stalls run along the two other walls, at panelling level. Three painted panels have been inserted into the wood, entitled by Hugo *LA FIN DU SEIGNEUR, LA FIN DU PRESTRE, LA FIN DU SOLDAT*. A mirror with an engraved decoration, similar to many other mirrors in the house, and crowned by a small cherub, reflects the fireplace.

The ceiling is decorated with a Gobelins tapestry, *L'Automne*. The series of four tapestries was bought by Victor Hugo on 27th September 1856. He used the fragments of one piece to adorn this very ceiling and placed the other two in the staircase. On one side, one can read in the panelling : *TU QUI TRANSIS PER DOMOS PERITURAS SIS MEM0R DOMUS AETERNAE* (You who pass through ephemeral abodes, do not lose sight of the final resting-place). Four carved panels depicting St. Anthony, St. Magdalen, the Holy Family and the Virgin and Child complete the decoration.

Around the table, six chairs bear the coats of arms of the Tuppers, an ancient Guernsey family, and their motto *L'ESPOIR EST MA FORCE*. Another features the arms of Victor Hugo.

From March 1862 on, a weekly meal was held here for deprived children. Initially there were only supposed to be twelve, but the number quickly rose to as high as forty, with half of them at a time coming to dine every week. On 5th March 1862, Victor Hugo noted : *I have made arrangements with Marie Sixty to carry out my idea of a meal for deprived children. Every week, twelve deprived children will dine in my house. They will be given the same food as us. We shall serve them. As they sit down, they will say : God be blessed. And as they rise : thanks be to God.* [...] And on 10th March : *The first dinner for the twelve deprived children took place here today. - We took a photograph.*

This initiative aroused wide interest and the idea was taken up in England. It was rounded off by a distribution of clothes and toys at Christmas, around a tree in the tapestry room.

Edmond Bacot
The dinner for deprived children
1862

To the left of the door as one leaves the room is the dumb waiter, which communicated with the kitchen in the basement.

At the bottom of the stairs, to the right of Auguste Vacquerie's former bedroom, the wooden panel bears the inscription *EDE I ORA* (Eat. Go. Pray), engraved on 22nd September 1859.

In October 1858, the flower print felt was laid in the hall and staircase leading to the first floor.

The doors on the right of the first-floor landing, hung with yellow and blue striped brocade, led to Mme Hugo and Adèle's bedrooms, now closed to the public.

The oeil-de-boeuf in its gilt frame, at the far end, was installed in March 1858. It is lit by a lamp named after one of Paul Meurice's plays, performed in November 1858. That same

Anon.

The dining room

year, on 21st December, Victor Hugo wrote in a letter to
Meurice : *I know your <u>Fanfan la Tulipe</u> is still flourishing. - At home
I have a tulip-shaped lamp to which I have given the glorious name
Fanfan.*

   Once more one notices the effect achieved by Victor
Hugo by placing two mirrors opposite one another, one on the
door at the far end, the other in the staircase.

   The red and blue drawing rooms lead off from the left.
These two showpieces, rich in Chinese curios, silks and gilding,
harking back to childhood memories in the Masserano palace in
Madrid, communicate with one another and form a kind of
gallery, over twelve meters long, flooded with light from the
garden.

1. Manuscript of the work *Chez Victor Hugo par un passant.*

THE RED DRAWING ROOM

There is an overall impression of opulence here, stemming from the red damask, furniture and gilt decor.

Against the far wall, four gilt wood *torchères*, standing on green painted rocks, frame the fireplace, and seem to be supporting a canopy draped in Chinese silk.

They go back to the pre-exile years, when they stood in the poet's apartment at 37, rue de la Tour-d'Auvergne, and were withdrawn from auction in June 1852. The Asiatic figures, in correspondingly inclined attitudes, carry torches upon which upturned candlesticks have been placed, bearing copper scales. They are on damask and red velvet plinths featuring the embroidered family coats of arms, Lorraine Hugos on the left and General Hugo on the right. In the background are two chimaera, identical to the ones in Juliette Drouet's Chinese drawing room, now preserved in the Maison de Victor Hugo.

On either side, standing on two higher plinths, are two red lacquer vases purchased in Brussels in the summer of 1863. These plinths, like those of the *torchères* in front, were part of a sedan chair which Victor Hugo had placed on the roof in June 1858, but which had to be brought down again in February 1860, following a hurricane.

Delft tiles depicting biblical scenes, similar to those in the dining room, cover the mantel of the fireplace. Just above is a metal belt adorned with garnet and green *cabochons* given to Victor Hugo by Sandor-Alexander Téléki, a Hungarian exile.

The copper brazier rests on a wooden plinth painted in red, with flowers drawn by Victor Hugo. The same decor features on the stepladder in the landing-library.

The embroidery on the armchair in the corner of the room is attributed to Mme Hugo. On the back are the family's coats of arms, topped by a helmet and Count's crown, outlined against the coat of peer of France (Victor Hugo had acceded to the peerage in 1845), itself topped by a Viscount's crown. In 1828, on General Hugo's death, Abel became Count, Eugene was granted the title of Viscount and Victor that of Baron. When Eugene died in 1837, the title of Viscount was handed down to Victor. Beneath the blazon is the motto *EGO HUGO*, in interwoven letters. The work was carried out after a drawing by Victor Hugo preserved in the Maison de Victor Hugo. On the cushion, a monogram of interwoven *Hs*, topped by the Viscount's crown, can be made out.

In the middle of the room, the marquetry table inlaid with ivory was bought in London by Charles Hugo in May 1859, along with the statues of St. Paul and St. John in the tapestry room.

Arsène Garnier
*Victor Hugo in the
red drawing room*
1868

The five embroidered panels on the walls and ceiling, including the one in the blue drawing room, contribute to the splendour of this decor. They were probably bought in Paris before the exile and the same technique has been applied to each of them, with metallic thread and chenille embroidery against a background of white glass pearls, dating back to the early XVIIIth century. They were probably made in England, but inspired by Oriental art. *This is pure needlework jewellery* wrote Charles Hugo[1]. On the wall, to the right of the door leading to the landing, a panel illustrates La Fontaine's fable *Le Coq et la Perle* (Book I, XX). The panel on the left is less easy to interpret. The ones on the ceiling are covered in a lush plant design.

A Murano chandelier, like the one in the blue drawing room, has replaced the gaslit globes used in Victor Hugo's day.

Lacquered panels, with a gilt decor on a red background on this side, separate the two rooms. They were formerly in the rue de la Tour-d'Auvergne in Paris, and were withdrawn from auction in June 1852.

1. CHARLES HUGO, *op. cit.*

Here again everything revolves around the fireplace, which has been positioned exactly opposite the one in the red drawing room. The reflection obtained by this play on mirrors is therefore multiplied into infinity.

The four spiral gilt columns may have been part of the four-poster bed owned by the poet in the rue de la Tour-d'Auvergne, which his daughter Adèle's diary tells us was withdrawn from auction in June 1852. A small silver platter has been inserted into the lintel. A mirror adorns the hearth. The fireplace, topped by an elaborate pediment in carved gilt wood, stands out against a panel bordered by a carved gilt frame made by Mauger in January 1859.

As in the red drawing room, the decor made much use of Chinese silk placed over the canopy and jambs of the fireplace, but this has since been replaced... *Bought the entire batch of Chinese silks sold by an English officer who took part in the*

expedition and removed them from the summer palace of the Chinese Emperor, wrote Victor Hugo on 23rd March 1865. The Chinese ceiling, in similar style which has since disappeared, was bordered by a frame carved by Mauger.

The walls of the alcoves were later covered in Chinese wallpaper, probably by the poet's grandchildren. The two convex *sorcière* mirrors were bought on 20th June 1860.

The armchair to the left of the fireplace, which features once again the motto *EGO HUGO*, was embroidered with the family coats of arms by Léopoldine Hugo in March-April 1843, shortly after she moved to Le Havre as a young bride. Her correspondence is studded with details of the work in progress, the colours used and the skeins she is constantly asking her mother to send. In a letter to Mme Paul Meurice, probably dated 13th August 1855, Adèle Hugo fondly recalls this memory :

Have you any idea, my dear friend, of the present state of the chair embroidered by my dear child ? As you know, it is an oak chair, with tapestry and velvet bands. - I would be much grieved if the work were to be destroyed, it would not be the least of the sacrifices of exile.

Victor Hugo bought the japanned pedestal table inlaid with tortoiseshell, to the right of the fireplace, on 29th June 1859.

The furniture includes two other lacquered items, one of which is a mirrored sideboard bought on 5th July 1859. The pagoda placed upon it is one of a pair purchased on 6th August 1860. The buddha seated on a throne, on the other sideboard, was bought a few days later.

Victor Hugo bought *the Amsterdam bench* opposite the windows in Holland in the summer of 1861. On 11th July 1862 he noted : *I have arranged for Grigg to paint and gild the Amsterdam bench [...]*. And almost two years later, on 24th March 1864 : *I have painted flowers and a coat of arms on the Amsterdam bench.*

In the centre of the room, on a table, is a lotus-shaped bronze incense-burner sent by Alexandre Dumas in April 1860 for a charity bazaar organised by Mme Hugo in aid of a crèche, and bought by Victor Hugo.

To complete the four pieces in the red drawing room, a panel embroidered with pearls, illustrating La Fontaine's fable *Le Geai paré des plumes du paon* (Book IV, IX), hangs on the wall above the *Amsterdam bench*. On the right, a panel depicting the Chinese god of longevity has been inserted into the door leading to the landing and placed between two glass panes in an antique carved gilt frame, introducing the same «slide» effect as between the tapestry room and studio.

The area was conducive to evenings with family and friends. On 25th February 1860 : *Performance of Charles' proverb <u>Trois contre une</u> in the blue room - began at 9.30 and finished at 11.15* and on 28th August of the same year : *This evening we performed Charles' comedy, <u>Je vous aime</u>, in the blue room. Charles, Victor,*

Anon.
*Victor Hugo in
the winter garden*

*M. Leballeur, Mlle Alphonsine and Allix. Audience : us, plus the usual
group.*

      A double glass door leads into the winter garden, a
verandah flooded with light, with an ideal view of the harbour.
The conservatory is finished. The divan installed wrote Victor Hugo
on 6th August 1859. In the summer he took some of his meals
here. There was a vine, providing grapes to eat on the spot. The
notebooks date the arrival of *the first vine plant in the conservatory*
as 15th May 1858 and on 18th January 1859 Victor Hugo noted :
*They are installing the iron trellis for the vine in the balcony
conservatory*. On the wall, the original wooden trellises outline
the letters *VH*.

      A staircase leads up to the second floor. Two large
carved panels, painted with coats of arms, originally from a ship,
stand out against the Dutch felt which covers the entire
stairwell. At the curve of the staircase, two Gobelins tapestries,

Anon.
The winter garden

Le Printemps and L'Eté, framed by Mauger in December 1858, cover the wall. A mirror topped by a cast-iron firescreen separates them. *They have hung the mirror at the top of the staircase and everything is more or less finished* noted Victor Hugo on 18th December 1858.

Until early 1862, a glass-panelled cone crowned the stairwell. At the end of 1861 and beginning of 1862, substantial work began in connection with the third-floor look-out. Victor Hugo had a glass room or look-out built above the eaves, communicating with his former study, which became the lobby of the look-out. The glass cone over the stairwell was removed and replaced by a transparent slab supported by a metal frame, forming the floor of the new look-out. Lamplight was made possible through the installation of gas pipes. The wooden drum which appears to encase the glass tile, together with its surrounding gilt frame, were laid in June 1862. On 29th May, Victor Hugo noted : *I have begun designing the rotunda for the staircase.*

This extraordinary composition, painted by the poet himself, calls upon a remarkable decorative repertoire on the theme of plants and flowers, reminiscent of the wooden frames painted for the billiard room in 1859 and his later design for the frame of the renowned *Burg à la Croix*, preserved in the Maison de Victor Hugo. The painted inscription *DEUS DIES* (God, Day) recurs, engraved on to a silver dish, above the mirror in the small staircase which leads to the third floor, with a frame painted by the poet along the same lines. By 9th July 1862 the work was completed : *Peter Mauger has taken down the scaffolding in the staircase.*

The visitor now reaches the second-floor landing. At the top of the stairs, on the left, is a montage of ten photographs taken by Charles Hugo and Auguste Vacquerie in Jersey, between 1852 and 1855. Their enthusiastic research into this new field of invention led them to produce a substantial number of prints, generally referred to as *the Jersey studio*. This montage provides a few examples : at the top centre Victor Hugo, with Adèle II on the left and Adèle I reading on the right ; in the centre, Victor Hugo on the exiles' rock, with his sons on either side, Charles on the left and François-Victor on the right ; at the bottom, Marine-Terrace, their Jersey home, in the centre, Léopoldine and her husband Charles Vacquerie on the left, and Auguste Vacquerie on the right, draped in a coat, and his cat. The collection is set within an ornate decor painted by Charles Hugo in 1855. At the centre of the composition, beneath the silk cartouche bearing the name *JERSEY*, four keys on a ring spell out the word *EXIL*. Each photograph is framed by architectural motifs highlighted in gilt paint. A number of captions accompany the documents, including a poem by Charles Hugo transcribed beneath the portraits of Léopoldine and Charles Vacquerie, who were drowned on 4th September 1843.

On the other wall, near a statue of St. Anne holding the Virgin and Infant Jesus, is a mirror painted by Charles Hugo, similar to the ones in the tapestry room.

The second-floor landing has been turned into a library. The glass-fronted shelves first installed in March 1858 still contain many works owned by Victor Hugo, including Diderot and d'Alembert's *Encyclopédie* (purchased in July 1860), Trevoux' *Dictionnaire* in five volumes (purchased in May 1862) and Moreri's *Dictionnaire historique*. As well as the frequent acquisitions of books registered in the notebooks throughout the exile years numerous works and leaflets were sent to

Victor Hugo. An inventory of the volumes in the library was carried out by Julie Chenay on 1st May 1863.

Once again, a mirror on the door of a glass cupboard catches the eye.

The red and gilt stepladder originally designed for the look-out was decorated with flowers and animals by Victor Hugo in February 1869 and painted by Tom Gor. On the outside of the left-hand jamb is the familiar double *H* of Hauteville House and on the transversal bar the letters *VH*.

In the foreground is a copying press ordered by the poet in late 1858.

Above a chiming clock is a variation of an old Latin motto, engraved into the wood : *TOUTES LAISSENT LEUR TRACE AU CORPS COMME A L'ESPRIT / TOUTES BLESSENT HELAS - LA DERNIERE GUERIT*.

The ceiling tapestry, with a fleur-de-lys pattern, laid on 11th June 1858, bears the monogram of Louis XIII and Anne of Austria.

To the right of the landing are two doors which used to lead to Charles and François-Victor's bedrooms, now closed to the public. The first is decorated with panels, probably of Portuguese origin. On 24th June 1858, Victor Hugo noted : *Bought an engraved plank from Forward to make Toto's door*. And two days later : *Gave Mauger the design for Victor's door*. The other door, in glass, has been adorned with a gilt frame, using the same technique as on the door at the far end and the door of the look-out lobby. Transparency and illusion come into play once more : the passage leading to the small staircase is topped by an empty gilt frame.

On 15th September 1859, on completion of the back library, containing Chippendale style furniture, Victor Hugo noted : *Little party. We danced in the gallery*.

Georges Hugo
Victor Hugo descending the staircase of the look-out

Heavy double doors covered with panels, also of Portuguese origin, and framed by spiral columns erected in May 1859, beneath a bas-relief depicting naiads, lead through from the left of the landing-library to the oak gallery. The two small carved heads at the base of the columns recall those carved by Mauger on the door of the dining room. Bottle bases are again used for decoration, as in the ground-floor entrance hall.

THE OAK GALLERY

The area referred to in the notebooks as *my study* or *my apartments* covers the surface of the two first-floor drawing rooms. The oak gallery, with two columns in the centre marking the entrance to the bedroom known as Garibaldi's room, involved substantial work, temporarily interrupted in January 1858 and taken up again until September 1859.

On this side, the carved and painted doors are decorated with figures of saints, including St. Peter, St. Paul and St. John the Baptist, originally partially gilded. On the lower part is the

André
*Victor Hugo
in the oak
gallery*
1878

inscription *PERGE SURGE* (Keep ahead. Arise) on a linen fold
background. On 13th August 1859, Victor Hugo noted : *I have
tried out the paint on the double doors of my study.* And on 29th
August : *I have traced and Mauger has gilded the inscription PERGE.
SURGE on the door of my apartments.*

On either side, two spiral columns complement those on
the landing and support a pediment graced with a small winged
head, installed by Mauger in March 1859. A chain, originally in
gilt, was attached to one of the columns in January 1861,
allowing the door to be closed from the inside.

In Victor Hugo's day, two tapestries hung in place of the
two panels in yellow damask on either side of the door. *La
Visitation* on the left and *La Rencontre d'Anne et de Joachim à
la Porte d'or* on the right. *L'Annonciation* was placed on the
same wall, above the leather bench, in Garibaldi's bedroom.

Here the walls and ceiling are concealed by wood
panelling and tapestries.

The far wall is in the spirit of the ground-floor drawing
room. In the centre, an imposing composition of carved and
crafted wood encases the fireplace. The blue and white Delft
tiles, with a Chinese statuette on them, relieve the general

Edmond Bacot
*The oak gallery
fireplace*
1862

austerity. *The oak fireplace is finished* noted Victor Hugo on
30th March 1858. The mirror, directly in line with the gallery, is
framed by large wooden caryatids supporting a coping
decorated with a carved panel. This probably depicts
Melchizedek and Abraham. On either side of the hearth, two
inscriptions were engraved on the base in September 1859 :
SUM / NON SEQUOR (I am and do not follow)* and *STO / SED
FLEO* (I am standing but weeping). In the upper corners of the
fireplace, the small carved wooden heads recall those in the
entrance hall and studio. The bearded figure placed in the
centre of the panel by Tom on 29th November 1859,
immediately above the mirror, is in totally different style.

The ensemble is completed to the left and right by
panels concealing cupboards and racks into which Victor Hugo
used to cram his personal papers, bonds and wills before
embarking on a journey... On the left, Portuguese panels, similar
to those in the gallery door on the landing, have been turned
into a cupboard door. Below, the carved panels evoke some of
the wood panelling on the ground-floor. The same Portuguese
panels turn up again on the right.

* Translator's note : a play on suis, which means both I am and I follow in French.

The wrought iron mantles adorned with a glass tulip-shaped lampshade have replaced the three-branch bracket lamps which used to gaslight the room. On 23rd March 1859 Victor Hugo noted : *The gas workmen have laid the pipes in my room. I have ordered the two bracket lamps for the fireplace from Morris.* And on 29th March : *The gas plumbers have installed the dragon (in my room). I lit the dragon this evening for the first time* [...]. He is referring to the small wooden dragon crowning the carved pediment of a cabinet placed between two windows.

To the right of the door, in the corner of the room, the *meuble à deux corps* entitled *the Burgos cupboard* is richly decorated with a mother of pearl and ivory inlay composed of animals and vases filled with lush foliate scrolls. A jade statuette crowns the pinnacle of the pediment and behind, on a brown leather panel, is a translation of one of Lucan's verses : *LES DIEUX / SONT / AU VAINQUEUR - CATON / RESTE / AUX VAINCUS*, in studded gold lettering. It seems more than likely that Victor Hugo designed the flower motif bordering this inscription. The gallery contains three panels of this kind, laid in November 1857.

Between two windows, the plinth of the small two-door sideboard against the wall is made from half a table, with spiral legs sawn off half-way up. The other half is situated between the windows in Garibaldi's room.

In February 1859, the three windows were decorated with lattice-work friezes designed by Victor Hugo and carved by Mauger. The initials of the poet appear once more, *V*, *VH*, *H*. The shutters, which Mauger made in late 1857, decorated with polychrome floral motifs, also feature the *V* and *H*.

In front of the fireplace is a heavy leaf-table, made by Mauger in November 1858 after a design by Victor Hugo. Mauger carved the winged heads which emerge from the corners.

The three armchairs are the product of Hugo's fertile imagination, and are in the spirit of the ancestors' armchair.

On 12th January 1859, the poet noted : *The large leather armchair is finished. I have written PATER behind it. I will write FILIUS behind the wooden armchair, and SPIRITUS behind the one with tapestry medals. All three will be placed around the large table.* The inscriptions stand out in studded lettering : *PATER, MATER* which replaced Spiritus, *FILIUS* to which the words *AMATUS AMAT* (Loved he loves) have been added, etched in a cartouche. In a letter addressed to his son Charles on 7th June 1862, Victor Hugo wrote : *Oh ! the day you are moved to write a complete work of art, you will know that your* Filius *chair is here, next to the* Pater *chair. It awaits you.*

In the centre, on a plinth made up of four carved panels depicting St. Peter, St. Matthew, St. Paul and St. Andrew, stands a large wooden candelabra created from drawings by Victor Hugo. It was installed in the gallery in May 1859. On 21st March 1859 he noted : *Gave Mauger instructions and the final design for the large wooden candelabra. I have given up the idea of putting in gas.* The candlesticks are in the shape of hollowed-out cotton reels. A statuette of the Virgin, carved by Victor Hugo in April 1859, stands on the top of the composition. *The large wooden candelabra I call <u>the tree of fire</u> was completed today 7th May* [1859].

Four wooden stalls, placed back-to-back in pairs, divide the oak gallery into two parts. On the left is a Gothic stall, its back decorated with a bas-relief beneath the Maison de France and Medici coat of arms. The stall on the right was made by Mauger after a design by Victor Hugo. On the back are the same saints as on the plinth of the tree of fire. In the centre, the figure of St. Peter is crowned with a small winged head and the inscription *A DEO AD DEUM* (From God. To God), engraved by Mauger in May 1859. The coat of arms of the Lorraine Hugos, framed by two gryphons, gives a discreet reminder of the owner's origins.

Two columns, erected in September 1857 and christened *TRISTITIA* and *LAETITIA* two years later by Victor Hugo, pave a majestic path to Garibaldi's room. The two

James Pradier
*Ivory head
used by
Victor Hugo
as the knob
of a cane*

inscriptions drawn by the poet can be made out on the base. The shafts, featuring a foliate scroll hung with bunches of grapes, were painted in asphalt in August 1859, one against a black background, the other against a red one. The Tristitia column was painted with silver and gold highlights which can still be seen today.

The heavy carved wood lintel, with pride of place given to a central convex mirror placed there in October 1857, completes the division of the gallery into two distinct parts. The two copper chandeliers, bought by Victor Hugo in Belgium in 1861 and personally shipped by him to Guernsey, along with a number of other purchases, were installed in September of that same year.

A large Flemish tapestry from XVIth century, *Le Jugement de Pâris*, trimmed with two cut-out fragments depicting Mercury and a female figure, cover the ceiling, completed in January 1858.

The following room is generally referred to as *Garibaldi's room*. The Italian patriot, with whom Victor Hugo had maintained an extremely cordial relationship since 1863, never actually visited Hauteville House despite an invitation from the poet, reiterated in *La Voix de Guernesey* (V), a long poem written and published in 1867 after the defeat at Mentana :

Nous, les proscrits d'Athènes, à ce proscrit de Sparte,
Ouvrons nos seuils ; qu'il soit notre hôte maintenant ;
Qu'en notre maison sombre il entre rayonnant.

Two stalls have been attached to the ones mentioned above. The one on the left, executed in November 1857, makes use of an already familiar decorative repertoire. The right-hand stall, with a panel cleverly concealing a cupboard door in the corner, is crowned by the coat of arms of General Léopold Hugo, framed by two gryphons. In the central back panel, a small carved wooden head emerges, similar to the ones on the dining room door and the entrance to the oak gallery on the landing.

Framed by two columns is a majestic four-poster bed. Two carved wood panels, one depicting tritons and naiads and the other a mask, make up the headboard, set against a marquetry background. The two little heads with flamboyant hair turn up again. This part was completed in November 1857. *I have had NOX MORS LUX engraved on the headboard of the main bed*, wrote Victor Hugo on 21st April 1859. The extraordinary ivory head which crowns the composition, representing the face of a bearded man when seen in left profile and a death's head in right profile, was carved by James Pradier, whom Victor Hugo knew well. A daughter, Claire, was born to Pradier and Juliette Drouet in 1826 but she died prematurely, like Léopoldine Hugo, at the age of twenty. On 26th September 1859, the notebooks comment : *Tom has placed the two-sided knob (used on a cane) given to me by Pradier in 1843 on the pinnacle of the headboard on my main bed.*

Four spiral columns, installed on 29th May 1857, support a canopy covered in floral and geometrical patterned panels. In Victor Hugo's day, it was also adorned with fabric-covered pelmets.

Elements from chests make up the sides of the bed. At the foot, between two statuettes, a panel depicts the sacrifice of Isaac. It may well come from what Victor Hugo *called the old Abraham chest* bought in June 1857.

An ingenious system of casters enables the bed to be moved lengthwise, closer to the two columns.

A close perusal of the notebooks makes it possible to measure the degree and length of the work involved, hindered by the inefficiency of the Guernsey workmen, as Victor Hugo never tired of pointing out. On 9th April 1859, for instance, one and a half years after the headboard was completed, he writes : *Jean has finished adjusting the main bed.*

On 27th December 1860, Victor Hugo noted : *night of 26th to 27th. I [...] slept in the main bed in the oak gallery for the first time. Appalling night. Insomnia. Fever.* Later the poet moved on to this floor on several occasions.

On either side of the bed are two alcoves which the workmen started converting in September 1857. The left-hand one housed the poet's dressing-room. The chest panel marking the entrance, decorated with two female sphinxes and supported by columns, was fitted in June 1858. On the back one can see the inscription *ERROR TERROR* in engraved gold lettering. The right-hand alcove conceals a small secret door opening on to the small staircase which leads to the look-out and enabled the poet to go directly to the third floor, which he had kept for himself.

Against the wall, on the left, is a large, somewhat composite item made from chests and known as the Guernsey sideboard. A panel, with a profile set in a medallion emerging from it, has been inserted into the upper part, framed by two small and distinct columns, one of which, decorated with lozenges, is reminiscent of the ones on the fireplace.

Above, a panel in studded leather adorned with flowers bears the inscription : *L'ESPRIT / SOUFFLE / OU / IL VEUT - L'HONNEUR / VA / OU / IL DOIT.*

One is struck by the strange sofa, also in studded leather. Two trunks were used to make the back and seat. The one on the back bears the initials of its former owner *SM*. They are completed by wooden elements covered in leather and decorated with studded motifs by Victor Hugo. On the lower part of the lateral jambs, gilt studs outline the double *V* above the arms of the Lorraine Hugos on the left, and the double *H* above those of the General on the right. *Mauger has completed the leather bench* wrote Victor Hugo on 21st November 1857. Later, in February-March 1859, Tom completed the ensemble, at the poet's request, by making the two leather-covered wooden racks on either side of the sofa in which Victor Hugo kept his documents.

On the right, *the Putiphar cupboard*, completed in October 1857, gets its name from the carved bas-relief depicting Joseph and Putiphar's wife. Two columns support an elaborate chest which makes up the upper part of the cupboard. They frame a leather-studded door highlighted with rich gilt motifs most probably taken from a wedding chest.

Above, the third leather-studded panel bears the inscription : *GLORIA / VICTIS - VAE / NEMINI* (Glory to the defeated. Harm to nobody).

On the ceiling, three *verdures*, completed by two small embroidered panels with mottoes, frame the canopy of the bed.

At the far end of the landing-library, a small staircase leads to the third floor where the poet could cut himself off and work in total peace.

The fretsawn mirror frame placed at the turn of the staircase was painted by Victor Hugo in April 1859. The visitor goes past the little secret door with lead cames leading to the oak gallery.

THE LOBBY AND LOOK-OUT

Edmond Bacot
The lobby and look-out
1862

A glass door leads through into the lobby of the look-out. On the right is a curious piece of furniture covered in velvet and fragments of tapestry known as the *Anne Boleyn piece* because of the interwoven initials *AB*. It was designed by Victor Hugo and executed in February 1859. The poet also designed the studded flowers which, on the sides, are exact replicas of some of the motifs in the oak gallery.

The entire room, including the sofas lining the walls, was covered in red and green flowered felt, some of it still visible today. For a long time, it served as the poet's study. He wrote the major part of *La Légende des siècles* here, at a small table with spiral legs, now preserved in the Maison de Victor Hugo, which he gave to Juliette Drouet on 16th August 1859.

Until late 1861, the area was enclosed, overlooking the glass cone which dominated the staircase. In September of the same year, Victor Hugo started looking into the idea of building a glass room on the roof. Work began in November. On 8th December 1861, shortly before publication of *Les Misérables*, the poet wrote to Auguste Vacquerie : *I am knee-deep in workmen, which makes my task even more arduous ; I am having a six-foot square crystal palace built on to my roof. I will install a small fireplace and small table, and have the sky and ocean to add zest.* Glazing was fixed on to the metal framework. On 28th December, Victor Hugo noted : *The carpenters have pulled down the gable façade and made the lobby of the look-out communicate with the glass room.* And the following day : *I have inaugurated the early stages of the glass room by reading a letter from JJ* [Juliette Drouet] *there.*

At the beginning of 1862, work continued with the removal of the glass cone and the laying of the look-out floor. The glass slab, which one can walk on, made of portholes which can be mechanically raised to allow for the cleaning of the chandelier, were only installed in the summer, along with the drum of the staircase.

The new glass room, overlooking the sea, became the poet's study. Victor Hugo started work very early in the morning. *I have worked in the crystal room for the first time, although it is far from finished* he noted on 2nd April 1862. The ideal location of the house creates a vast panorama from this point, with the harbour and Cornet Castle in the foreground. Victor Hugo actually witnessed the building of the jetty linking the castle to land, and crossed it himself for the first time on 23rd May 1860.

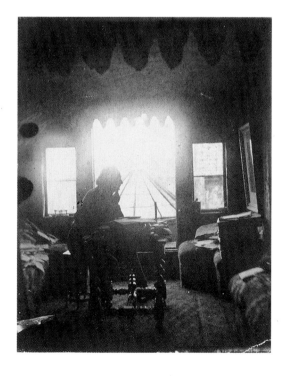

Anon.
*Victor Hugo
in his study
before the
construction of
the look-out*

Two sofas face one another. They were placed there in January 1862 and covered with rugs. On the wall in the entrance three mirrors reflect the harbour.

Under the window-frame, flanked by a carved wooden frieze decorated with birds, butterflies and flowers, the far wall was covered with plaques and purple, blue and white Delft tiles in February 1862. The poet supervised the layout extremely closely. The white china stove in the centre, on blue tiling, provided the heating for this room, much exposed to cold and inclement weather. On 18th October 1862, Victor Hugo noted : *For the first time I made a fire in the fireplace-stove in the crystal room, and worked there from seven o'clock in the morning.*

Two table-flaps can be seen at either end, at which the poet wrote standing, facing the sea. All his life Victor Hugo kept up this habit, which he had already adopted in the place Royale, before his exile. On 25th December 1858, the following comment occurs in the notebooks : *I have gone back to the idea of having a desk made for my study so that I can write standing up.* The furniture from the poet's bedroom in the avenue d'Eylau mansion in Paris, where he spent his final years, is now preserved in the Maison de Victor Hugo, and includes a high desk made up of two superposed tables.

On 25th December 1863, Victor Hugo wrote to Auguste Vacquerie : *I am working a great deal. This is the positive aspect of exile. The days are short, I get up at dawn. I have a crystal room overlooking the sea. Its roar intermingles with my work.*

This is where Victor Hugo completed *Les Misérables* and wrote *William Shakespeare*, *Les Travailleurs de la mer*, *Mille francs de récompense*, the introduction to *Paris Guide*, *Mangeront-ils* ?, *L'Homme qui rit* and *Quatrevingt-treize*. On 21st November 1872, he comments : *Today I begin the book* Quatrevingt-treize *(First tale). In my crystal room, I have before me the portrait of Charles and the two portraits of Georges and Jeanne.*

I got out the new crystal inkstand bought in Paris and opened a brand-new bottle of ink [...], took a ream of watermarked paper bought especially for this book, took a familiar old pen and began writing the first page.

Georges Hugo, the poet's grandson, who in 1878, at the age of ten, accompanied his grandfather to Guernsey, later recalled the experience : *I can still see him climbing the dark staircase, laid from wall to wall with thick felt in a rose and dead leaf pattern, with his measured, increasingly heavy tread : with one hand in*

Edmond Bacot
Victor Hugo's study
1862

the pocket of his trousers and the other leaning heavily on the banister, he was on his way to work. [...]

He entered the «look-out», a roof-top conservatory with no blinds, which let in the searing blue sky reflected by the sea, and at a small flap desk, before a mirror decorated by him with a flower composed of strange petals, its silvering blistered and cracked by the heat, he wrote[1].

Two doors provide access to the roof. On the right-hand corner of the balcony, Victor Hugo used to hang out an early morning signal for Juliette Drouet, who had been living in Hauteville Fairy since June 1864, to reassure her that he had slept well. *Today, as I got up, I introduced the habit of placing a white signal on the corner of my balcony, which she can see from her new home* noted Victor Hugo on 15th July 1864. This is the impatiently awaited *torchon radieux* (radiant cloth) Juliette refers to in her letters. The expression originates from a poem in *Les Chansons des rues et des bois* (Book I, IV, 7) :

Sachez qu'hier, de ma lucarne,
J'ai vu, j'ai couvert de clins d'yeux
Une fille qui dans la Marne
Lavait des torchons radieux.

1. G. VICTOR HUGO, *Mon grand-père*, Paris, 1902.

André
*Victor Hugo
in the look-out*
1878

VICTOR HUGO'S BEDROOM

A small corridor still partially hung with the same green and red-flowered felt opens into the lobby of the look-out and leads to Victor Hugo's bedroom. *I am getting the corridor of the look-out laid out (by Mauger)* wrote Victor Hugo on 19th June 1859. Despite its poky dimensions, the poet allowed his imagination a free rein. A lacquered cabinet was inserted into the partition separating the corridor from a small room reserved for the servants. *I have moved into the look-out, right on top of the house ; it is a cell overlooking the sea* [...]. (Night of 6th to 7th December 1856). The poet actually used the same term, look-out, to describe the small third-floor bedroom with its belvedere overhanging the garden.

Work began in September 1858 on this room, which is surprisingly plain and narrow. The walls and ceiling are hung with yellow fabric. There is neither a fireplace nor a stove, although the room is extremely exposed to rain and wind. *I have taken up my work again in the fireless look-out overlooking the garden (my bedroom)* is the comment in the notebooks on 31st March 1865.

Underneath a mirror, a sofa covered in velvet and silk occupies the far end of the room. Hallucinations and disturbed dreams often disrupted Victor Hugo's sleep and he regularly altered the position of his bed. In 1865, he decided to move into François-Victor's room : *My nights are too disturbed by this singular obsession. I have decided to sleep in Victor's room* [...]. (19th February 1865).

Two cabinets stand on table-tops adorned with lambrequins. The processional cross, which already belonged to Victor Hugo before his exile, was used as the model for his great drawing, *Le Burg à la Croix*, preserved in La Maison de Victor Hugo.

On the wall are portraits of Léopoldine and Charles Vacquerie by Mme Hugo, with an inscription underneath by Victor Hugo : *toujours vivants / là-haut et en moi.* Another portrait of Léopoldine, drawn by her mother in 1847, four years after the Villequier drama, has been placed here.

On the floor in front of the sofa are two terracotta figurines of children, which Victor Hugo had gilded in 1861.

The two panels inserted into the wood on either side of the window were drawn and painted by Victor Hugo and show clear similarities with the decor of the Chinese drawing room in Hauteville Fairy, reconstituted in the Maison de Victor Hugo. The left-hand one conceals the china basin at which the poet conducted his morning ablutions in cold water, when he was not carrying out *hydrotherapy* on the roof. *Yesterday and today I designed the two large dragon panels for my look-out* he noted on 10th March 1864. Gor installed them in November of the same year.

These panels fired the imagination of Georges Hugo : *They tell the story of a beauty, a knight and a beast. The drawings intrigued us to such an extent that we sometimes made Papapa come into the room and recount them. And he would tell us how the knight, who was in love with the beauty, needed to kill the dragon and bring her its head before she would love him in return. In words as well as pictures, he described the fight between the knight and the monster with its hooked claws, its ringed tail quivering with rage ; how the lover, astride a mythological bird, killed the dragon by plunging his sword straight into its mouth. Then, before the beauty's elegant form [...], he described the ardour of the kneeling young warrior [...] We then delighted at the death of the dragon, whose severed head [...] hung from the knight's outstretched arm*[1].

From his window, the poet could see Juliette Drouet, who had moved into La Fallue, now an hotel, in December 1857. Victor Hugo supervised the lengthy conversion work on the house, and in 1857 sent Mauger to work for Juliette. The notebooks register a number of purchases of chests and objects specifically for the house. On 8th November 1857, Juliette Drouet wrote : [...] *I have to tell you, from my very soul, how touched, honoured, overwhelmed, grateful, moved and happy I am by all the trouble you have taken these past three months to furnish me with a miniature domestic paradise.*

Some of the pieces of furniture designed by Victor Hugo for Juliette Drouet are on display in the Maison de Victor Hugo.

Poor health forced Juliette to leave her house for Hauteville Fairy, just a few doors away from Hauteville House. In June 1864 she reluctantly moved in. On 2nd March 1864, she wrote : [...] *I am in no rush to enter this Paradise and the nearer I get to the fatal moment the more I long to postpone it, so attached am I to my dear little house, from which I can see yours* [...]. The remarkable Chinese decor, now exhibited in the Place des Vosges, was conceived by Victor Hugo for Hauteville Fairy.

Hauteville House has therefore been preserved as a haven of memories, where the poet's grandchildren stayed from their earliest childhood.

In the summer of 1870, as a result of the action taken against *Le Rappel*, Charles Hugo, who had not been back to Guernsey since July 1863, returned with Alice and their children. The latter went back again in summer 1872 and during Victor Hugo's last visit in 1878.

Upon his death, the house was handed down to Georges and Jeanne.

In March 1927, the centenary of the Romantic movement, it was donated to the Ville de Paris by Jeanne Hugo and Georges' children, Jean, Marguerite and François. This gesture respected the wish formulated by Georges in July 1914, during the unveiling of the poet's statue in Guernsey. In June 1927, a formal ceremony in the presence of the family and a number of representatives from both Paris and Guernsey officially handed over the house to the Ville de Paris, and its collections became a precious adjunct to those of the museum in the place des Vosges.

1. G. VICTOR HUGO, *op. cit.*

Valentin Guillon
*Victor Hugo,
Georges and Jeanne
in the garden*
1878

Arsène Garnier
*Victor Hugo
in the garden*
1868

1802   Victor Hugo born in Besançon (26th February).

1803   Adèle Foucher born. Léopold Hugo takes his three
        sons to Corsica, and then to Elba where Sophie joins them.

1804   Sophie and her sons return to Paris : rue Neuve-des-Petits-
        Champs, then rue de Clichy.

1806   Birth of Juliette Gauvain, the future Juliette Drouet.

1808   Sophie and the children join Léopold in Naples.

1809   Sophie and the children return to Paris : rue de Clichy,
        then rue Saint-Jacques, then impasse des Feuillantines.

1811   Sophie and the children join Léopold in Madrid.
        Eugène and Victor become boarders at Nobles college.

1812   Sophie, Eugène and Victor return to Les Feuillantines.

1813   Sophie and the children move into the rue des Vieilles-Tuileries.

1815   Eugène and Victor become boarders at the pension Cordier.
        Victor begins his *Cahiers de vers français*.

1816   *La France en deuil*. *Le Déluge*. *Irtamène*. Lessons at the lycée
        Louis-le-Grand.

1817   Awarded a distinction by the Académie Française for his
        competition entry, the poem *Du bonheur que procure l'étude
        dans toutes les situations de la vie*. Victor begins *Athélie* and
        writes *A.Q.C.H.E.B.* (A quelque chose hasard est bon).

1818   First draft of *Bug-Jargal* (published in 1820).

1819   Obtains Lys d'or (golden lily award) at the Toulouse Académie des
        Jeux Floraux for his ode on *Le Rétablissement de la statue de
        Henri IV*. The *Conservateur littéraire* is founded. *Inez de Castro*.

1820   Granted royal gratuity for his ode on *La mort du duc de
        Berry*. Sophie and her children move into the rue de
        Mézières. Ode on *La Naissance du duc de Bordeaux*.

1821   Victor begins *Han d'Islande* (published in 1823). Death of
        Sophie Hugo. Engagement of Victor and Adèle.

1822   Victor moves into the rue du Dragon. Awarded royal grant
        following publication of *Odes et Poésies diverses*. Adèle and
        Victor married at the church of Saint-Sulpice and set up home
        at 39, rue du Cherche-Midi.

1823   Beginning of *La Muse française*. A son, Léopold-Victor, is
        born, but survives less than three months.

1824   *Nouvelles Odes*. Move to 90, rue de Vaugirard.
        Léopoldine born.

1825   Victor made chevalier de la Légion d'honneur. Travels to Reims
        for the Anointment of Charles X. Ode on *Le Sacre de Charles X*.

1826   Publication of the second version of *Bug-Jargal*, and *Odes et
        Ballades*. Charles born.

1852	Expelled from France by decree. Furniture auctioned in Paris. *Napoléon-Le-Petit* published in Brussels. Leaves for Jersey. Moves into Marine-Terrace.
1853	Takes up spiritualism. *Châtiments*.
1854	*Lettre à Lord Palmerston*. Hugo composes some sections of *La Fin de Satan*.
1855	Hugo composes part of *Dieu*. Expelled from Jersey. Arrives in Guernsey.
1856	*Les Contemplations*. Buys Hauteville House.
1857	Short visit paid by Alexandre Dumas. Juliette Drouet moves into La Fallue.
1858	*La Pitié suprême*, *L'Ane* (published in 1879 and 1880). First of the Adèles' Paris visits.
1859	The Adèles spend time in London. Hugo refuses amnesty. *La Légende des siècles*. Intervenes in favour of John Brown.
1860	Adèle I goes to Paris. Victor Hugo makes short visit to Jersey. Takes up *Les Misérables* again.
1861	Adèle I returns to Paris, then to Brussels with her daughter. Victor Hugo travels to Belgium and Holland.
1862	Adèle I goes to Paris. First meal for deprived children. *Les Misérables*. Victor Hugo travels to Belgium, Luxembourg and the Rhine.
1863	*Victor Hugo raconté par un témoin de sa vie*. Repeated visits to Paris by Adèle I. Adèle II flees to Halifax. Victor Hugo travels to Luxembourg, the Rhineland and Belgium. *Chez Victor Hugo par un passant* by Charles Hugo.
1864	*William Shakespeare*. Juliette Drouet moves into Hauteville Fairy. Victor Hugo travels to the Ardennes and the Rhineland. Adèle I returns to Guernsey after an absence of over sixteen months.
1865	Adèle I settles in Brussels. Victor Hugo visits Brussels. Travels to Germany and Luxembourg. Marriage of Charles and Alice Lehaene in Brussels. *Les Chansons des rues et des bois*.
1866	Drafts *Mille francs de récompense*. *Les Travailleurs de la mer*. Visits Brussels. Adèle II leaves for Barbados.
1867	Adèle I makes brief visit to Guernsey. Drafts *Mangeront-ils ?* Publication of *Paris Guide* (with an introduction by Victor Hugo). Visits Brussels. Travels to Zeeland. *La Voix de Guernesey*.
1868	Visits Brussels. Georges, Charles' son, born. Adèle I dies in Brussels. Victor Hugo accompanies her coffin as far as the French border.

1869	Drafts *L'Epée*. *L'Homme qui rit* published. Le *Rappel* founded. Drafts *Torquemada* (published in 1882). Visits Brussels. President of the Peace Congress. Jeanne, Charles' daughter, born.
1870	Charles and his family visit Guernsey. Hugo returns to France (5th September). Moves in with Paul Meurice. First French edition of *Châtiments*.
1871	Elected Paris deputy and joins the Assembly in Bordeaux, but resigns one month later. Death of Charles. Stays in Brussels and then in Vianden.Back in Paris, moves into 66, rue de la Rochefoucauld.
1872	Adèle II returns to Paris. Revival of *Ruy Blas*. *L'Année terrible*. Spends a year in Guernsey.
1873	Moves in with François-Victor for three months in Auteuil, then to 55, rue Pigalle. Death of François-Victor.
1874	*Quatrevingt-treize*. Moves to 21, rue de Clichy. *Mes Fils*.
1875	Spends a week in Guernsey. *Actes et Paroles* I and II (*Avant l'exil - Pendant l'exil*). Literary testament.
1876	Elected senator. *Actes et Paroles* III (*Depuis l'exil*).
1877	2nd series of *La Légende des siècles*, *L'Art d'être grand-père*, *L'Histoire d'un crime* (1st part).
1878	*L'Histoire d'un crime* (2nd part), *Le Pape*. Stroke. Spends four months in Guernsey. Moves into 130, avenue d'Eylau.
1879	Visits Veules-les-Roses and Villequier.
1880	*Religions et religion*.
1881	Celebration to mark Victor Hugo's eightieth year. *Les Quatre vents de l'esprit*. Draws up his will.
1882	Visits Veules-les-Roses.
1883	Death of Juliette Drouet. 3rd series of *La Légende des siècles*. Adds codicil to will. *L'Archipel de la Manche*.
1884	Travels to Switzerland.
1885	Death of Victor Hugo (22nd May). State funeral.

Family tree

Léopold HUGO
1773-1828
1st wife Sophie TRÉBUCHET 1772-1821
2nd wife Catherine THOMAS 1783-1858

by 1st marriage

Abel
1798-1855
m. Julie DUVIDAL de MONTFERRIER
1797-1865

Eugène
1800-1837

Victor
1802-1885
m. Adèle FOUCHER
1803-1868

Léopold
1823

Léopoldine
1824-1843
m. Charles VACQUERIE
1817-1843

Charles
1826-1871
m. Alice LEHAENE
1847-1928
remarried in 1877
Edouard LOCKROY

François-Victor
1828-1873

Adèle
1830-1915

Georges
1867-1868

Georges
1868-1925
1st wife Pauline MENARD-DORIAN
2nd wife Dora DORIAN
by 1st marriage by 2nd marriage

Jeanne
1869-1941
1st husband Léon DAUDET
2nd husband Jean CHARCOT
3rd husband Michel NEGREPONTE
by 1st marriage

Jean
1894-1984

Marguerite
1896-1984

François
1899-1982

Charles
1892-1960

VISITOR'S ENTRANCE

Hauteville House
38 Hauteville
St. Peter Port. Guernsey
Channel Islands
Tel. (481) 72 19 11

HOURS OF OPENING

10.00 to 11.30 and 14.00 to 16.30
Open daily from 1st April to 30th September
Closed on Sundays and local public
holidays (4th April, 2nd, 9th and 30th May,
29th August)

Guided tours only available in groups of 15
Advance booking possible

Guide written by :
Sophie Grossiord, Curator at the Maison de Victor Hugo

Graphic design : Gilles Beaujard

Layout : Viviane Linois

Production : Florence Jakubowicz

English translation : Caroline Taylor-Bouché

Photogravure : Fotimprim, Paris

Flashing : Delta +, Paris

Printing : Imprimerie Alençonnaise, Paris

First printed by imprimerie Alençonnaise in Alençon, March 1994

Cover : *The dining-room fireplace at Hauteville House*

Photographic acknowledgments :
Photothèque des musées de la Ville de Paris, © by SPADEM 1994
Photo : Rémi Briant, Philippe Joffre, Philippe Ladet, Jean-Marc Moser,
Patrick Pierrain, Jean-Yves Trocaz, D.R.